BOOK ANALYSIS

Written by Éléonore Quinaux
Translated by Rebecca Neal

The Girl on the Train

BY PAULA HAWKINS

PAULA HAWKINS

BRITISH NOVELIST

- **Born in Harare (Zimbabwe) in 1972.**
- **Notable works:**
  - *Hot Property* (2001), practical guide
  - *The Money Goddess* (2006), practical guide
  - *Into the Water* (2017), novel

Paula Hawkins was born and grew up in Zimbabwe, before moving to London with her family in 1989. Her father is an economics professor, and she followed in his footsteps to an extent by studying philosophy, politics and economics at Oxford University. She worked as an economics journalist for *The Times* and published a number of financial guides, such as *The Money Goddess* (2006), before turning her hand to fiction in 2009.

She initially wrote romantic fiction under the pseudonym Amy Silver, before publishing the psychological thriller *The Girl on the Train* in 2015. The novel was a dazzling success, topping bestseller lists around the world and being adapted into a hit film. Hawkins has previously lived in France and Belgium, and is currently based in London.

THE GIRL ON THE TRAIN

A POLYPHONIC THRILLER

- **Genre:** novel
- **Reference edition:** Hawkins, P. (2016) *The Girl on the Train*. London: Transworld.
- **1st edition:** 2015
- **Themes:** murder, anxiety, psychology, psychopaths, London, adultery, alcoholism, domestic violence

The Girl on the Train was published in 2015 and is Paula Hawkins' first novel under her own name. Inspired by commuters from outer London, Hawkins tells the story of a desperate, disillusioned, alcoholic young woman who lives vicariously through the seemingly perfect couple she sees from the train every day and eventually gets tangled up in their lives for real when she witnesses an affair and learns of a murder.

The atmosphere of the novel is tense but not stifling, and the reader follows the feelings, ideas and thoughts of multiple characters, as the chapters focus on each of them in turn. As a result, the story and the reading experience often unfold at the same pace.

SUMMARY

DREAM OR NIGHTMARE?

Rachel, a young woman who lives just outside London, has been drinking heavily for several years, with dire consequences: she has lost her job, her marriage has ended in divorce, and her life is miserable. However, she does not want her friend and landlady Cathy to find out about this, so she takes the train to London every day with the other commuters and pretends to be going to work. Every day, she goes past her old home in Witney and daydreams about what could have been if her ex-husband Tom had not cheated on her with Anna, who he has since married. Her attention is also drawn to a Victorian-style house on the same street and the seemingly perfect couple who live there. Every time the train goes past the house, Rachel observes the couple: she has named them Jess and Jason, and imagines their life as a way of coming to terms with the ideal that she has lost. But could Rachel's old life ever have been as good as she wanted it to be?

The murder of Jess, who was really called Megan, tarnishes the image of the perfect neighbourhood and of Rachel's ex-husband Tom, however perfect he may seem from the outside. Although Tom acts like the ideal man and paints Rachel as an alcoholic who tore their marriage apart, driving him into the arms of a mistress, over the course of the story we learn that he is both a consummate manipulator and a murderer. Tom seems kind, charming and fun to be around, but is a serial philanderer: after cheating on Rachel, he does the same to his second wife. He comes up with excuses, claiming that he is playing sports, on business trips or meeting up with his old army friends – even though he has never been a soldier – while he is really seeing other women.

However, it all started to unravel for him when one of his mistresses, his neighbour Megan, fell pregnant, told her husband Scott (the man Rachel calls Jason) about the affair and told Tom that she did not want to have an abortion. One day in July 2013, Tom and Megan were talking in the woods when their conversation turned acrimonious. Tom flew into a rage, picked up a rock and hit Megan with it, killing her. The investigators only discovered her body a few days later, when it was uncovered by the rain and mudslides.

AN UNRELIABLE WITNESS

The day before the murder, Rachel took her train in the morning and watched Jess in her garden. Jess was with an olive-skinned man who was not her husband and who hugged her. Rachel is haunted by thoughts about who the other man could be.

Rachel starts drinking, as she often does, and cannot stop herself from calling Tom, who she is still in love with, loitering outside the house they used to share (and where he still lives) and growing aggressive towards him and his wife Anna. Furthermore, when she drinks there are always long gaps in her memory afterwards. She knows that she was drunkenly wandering around her old neighbourhood the night Jess/Megan was murdered, that she saw Tom there, and that the next day she was covered in cuts, bumps and bruises.

There is just one problem: she cannot remember

anything else about that fateful night. Nothing seems to fit or match up in her mind. Rachel then decides to embark on her own inquiry, independent of the police investigation. She insinuates herself into the victim's husband Scott's life by pretending to be a friend of Megan's. She helps him to uncover Megan's affair for himself, while she manages to identify Megan's olive-skinned lover as her therapist Kamal Abdic. Rachel is determined to get to the bottom of the case and goes to see Abdic in order to get a better idea about this man with a warm voice but an icy smile. She then goes to the police station and identifies him as the man who was in Megan's garden.

But who is going to believe an alcoholic? The police are dismissive of Rachel's claims, particularly when Scott discovers that she lied to him and that she had never known Megan. Left without allies, the success of Rachel's investigation now hinges on her alone, even as she continues to battle her amnesia.

THE CHARMING PSYCHOPATH

Although Rachel initially saw the therapist as the most likely culprit, her suspicions then turn towards Jason, Megan's jealous, violent husband, who also lashed out at Rachel herself on one occasion. However, as the investigation takes a stronger hold over her than alcohol, Rachel gradually starts drinking less and fills in the gaps in her memory from her drunken blackouts. She realises that when she was married to Tom, he constantly lied to her and abused her before accusing her of attacking him, confident in his belief that she would not remember exactly what happened.

On the evening of the murder, she was right next to Megan's house, in a little tunnel leading to the train station, and she suddenly remembers seeing Tom in his red car. He was not alone. For a long time, Rachel had believed that he was with Anna, but then her memory comes back and she realises that it was actually Megan in the car next to him. Gradually, the fog clears: Rachel remembers that Tom was furious that she had come to the house for the umpteenth time, and dragged her into the street and beat her savagely.

As she realises that it is more than likely that her ex-husband is the murderer, she goes to his house to warn Anna that she and her baby are in danger. Fortunately for Rachel, Tom is not there and she is able to tell Anna everything she knows. Anna, who had previously thought that she was untouchable, has recently begun to suspect that Tom is cheating on her. She found a phone that does not belong to him among his things, and it turns out to be Megan's. This means that when Rachel comes to tell her that Tom is a philanderer and compulsive liar, for once Anna does not turn her away and actually hears her out.

However, Tom suddenly appears. Backed into a corner by the two women, he admits that he killed Megan and seems ready to murder Rachel too. Fortunately, she manages to get a corkscrew out of a drawer and fatally stabs Tom with it. She is not charged for the murder because Anna tells the authorities that she acted in self-defence (although she did not come to her aid when Tom attacked her). Megan, whose name had been dragged through the mud by the newspapers, is laid to rest in peace. Rachel can then rebuild her life, and has no further contact with Scott and Anna.

CHARACTER STUDY

RACHEL WATSON

Rachel is 34 and has always worked in public relations. However, she is an alcoholic and lost her job because of her behaviour when under the influence. Since then, she has become depressed and takes the train from Ashbury, Buckinghamshire to Euston every day in order to pretend that she is still working. She lives with an old university friend, Cathy, who she had previously lost touch with.

Although she is divorced from Tom Watson, who calls her Rach, she kept his surname to avoid the hassle of changing all her documents – and above all because she still loves him. She lived with him for five years in a Victorian house in Witney, at 23 Blenheim Road. She was left heart-broken when she failed to conceive, even after IVF, and turned to drink to deal with her feelings. To begin with, this made her more outgoing, but then she turned aggressive and her behaviour spiralled out of control.

She is fat, has a haggard appearance and is bloated from her drinking, so she is no longer young and pretty like she was when she was married to Tom. She wants to escape her miserable, depressing existence and whiles away the time inventing stories about the people she sees from the train window. These include Megan and Scott (who she names Jess and Jason), who she sees as the perfect couple and who fill her with curiosity.

Absorbed by the story of the murder and the investigation she is carrying out to get to the bottom of it, Rachel stops drinking and finds work as a secretary through Cathy. She gets her confidence back, starts thinking more clearly and realises that Tom treated her as his punchbag throughout their entire relationship. She is talkative, dynamic, impulsive, interfering and sometimes thoughtless when she has been drinking, but she is a good person at heart. As her father is dead and her mother neglects her and pays little attention to her struggles, Rachel knows that the only person she can count on is herself. She is the one who identifies Megan's murderer and drives the plot forward.

TOM WATSON

Tom Watson is Rachel's ex-husband. He is a serial philanderer and left Rachel for his mistress Anna, who he then married. They have a daughter, Evie, together. Tom works as a property expert and is a handsome man, although his skin is pale and his eyes are a little too close together. He seems to be above suspicion, as he is a kind and loving husband and is even nice to Rachel, who keeps harassing him.

However, in his case appearances are deceptive: Tom is actually a manipulative liar. He claims that he was in the army and still has friends who are soldiers, but in reality he was too mentally unstable to serve. He constantly has affairs and is a compulsive liar. He is a fundamentally violent man: during his first marriage, he regularly hit Rachel, using her drinking problem and alcohol-induced forgetfulness to convince her that she attacked him first and he had no choice but to defend himself.

He has money problems and uses this as an excuse to avoid selling the house he used to share with Rachel. This disappoints Anna, who is desperate to move. He claims that the money they would get from the house, which has lost value because it is next to the railway, would not be enough for them to find somewhere else, unless they had an additional source of income. In reality, Tom is attached to the house where he committed his first misdeeds. In addition, neither of his wives has met his parents, and he seems very reluctant to introduce them. He does not want to admit to Rachel or Emma that he is no longer on speaking terms with his parents, as he had forced them to mortgage their house to fund his lifestyle.

Although he seems to be a good father to his daughter Evie in public, Anna is the one who really looks after her. She is helped by Megan, Tom's mistress, who he brought into the family home as Evie's nanny. Tom ends up killing Megan so that she does not tell Anna about their affair, and above all because he does not want her to keep their child.

SCOTT HIPWELL

Scott is a 36-year-old self-employed IT consultant. He lives with his wife Megan at number

15 on Tom and Anna's street. Scott has brown hair, is taller than Tom and is physically strong. He is jealous by nature and is psychologically abusive towards Megan, monitoring everything she does. He is hot-headed, is quick to anger and breaks things when he is worked up. He is worried about his wife's health and encourages her to see a therapist. He is madly in love with Megan and, unlike her, is happy that she is not working any more.

Rachel insinuates herself into his life during the investigation, and even becomes a friend who he confides in. However, he pushes her away when he finds out that she was only pretending to be Megan's friend to get close to him. From then on, Scott's only source of support is his overbearing mother.

The day before his wife was murdered, Scott had a violent argument with her and almost strangled her. He had dreamed of being a father and cannot come to terms with the idea that the child Megan is carrying is not his. For a long time, he is a key suspect in his wife's murder, and he lets himself go: he stops washing, drinks heavily and turns violent, in particular towards Rachel.

Throughout the investigation, he is harassed by photographers, journalists and the police, who see him as the most likely culprit.

MEGAN HIPWELL

Megan, nicknamed Megs, was born in Rochester and is Scott's wife. Other people see her as very beautiful: she is slender, with blue eyes and long blond hair. However, she seems unable to maintain a stable relationship: although she loves her husband, she cannot stop herself from meeting up with other men to stave off boredom in her long, inactive days, only partially occupied by Pilates classes and time spent with her friend Tara. She used to run an art gallery in Witney which went bankrupt, and looks for ways to fill her time, in particular by applying for a fabrics course at St Martins.

She also occupies herself for several months by looking after Tom and Anna's daughter Evie, but she cannot stand the baby. This can be explained by the fact that her older brother, Ben, who she had planned to travel the world with, was killed by an articulated lorry at the age of just 19. Megan's world was turned upside down, and after the funeral she ran away, sought refuge in drugs and lost contact with her parents, who died without ever reconciling with her. When she was 16, Megan met Craig McKenzie, known as Mac, who was older than her, and fell pregnant a year later. Then, tragedy struck: in a drugged haze, Megan fell asleep and forgot about her baby, Libby, who was in the bath and drowned.

Megan has told nobody, not even Scott, about her pregnancy and the death of her baby. She ends up revealing her secrets to her therapist, Kamal Abdic, with whom she is having an affair. She has also been Tom's mistress for the past several months, and falls pregnant. Her refusal to get an abortion has fatal consequences for her: Tom kills her by hitting her in the head with a rock. She is buried in Scotland near her daughter.

ANNA WATSON

Anna is Tom's second wife and Evie's mother. She has blond hair and a dimple in her left cheek when she smiles. She is an estate agent and met her future husband at work, where they embarked on an affair. Anna misses that period of her life, because being Tom's mistress was more exciting than her current life as a housewife. She goes along with Tom's suggestion and lets Megan help her look after Evie, although she has never understood why Tom thought it necessary.

Anna is bad-tempered, never feels compassion and hates Rachel, as she is fed up with her constant calls and intrusions into her life. She is scared of what Tom's ex-wife will do next, and wants to take out a restraining order against her. She also makes sure that the police attach no credibility to Rachel's account by telling the investigators that she is an alcoholic. She becomes suspicious when she notices that her husband is paying less and less attention to her. She is selfish, calculating and passionate, and she is slow to grasp that she will need to help Rachel to get rid of her husband if she wants to save her own skin. When she is questioned after Tom's death, she saves the woman who was her enemy only a short time before by saying that she acted in self-defence.

ANALYSIS

A THREE-PART NARRATIVE

The narration of *The Girl on the Train* makes it a somewhat unusual novel. Three female characters give us their version of events, day after day: Rachel, Megan and Anna. Their reactions and comments follow on from their thoughts, and do not necessarily appear in chronological order (for example, the dead Megan goes back over the events which preceded her death). We therefore do not read three perfectly linear stories, but rather three points of view on the same plot which are constantly shifting as the protagonists discover new information.

As an illustration, Rachel's point of view, which is initially fuzzy because she is drinking too much and running away from her life, becomes increasingly clear as she fills in the gaps in her memory. Meanwhile, Anna starts off as a loving wife and former mistress who paints an idyllic picture of her relationship with Tom and sees Rachel as an enemy to be defeated, but this all changes when she realises the inconsistencies in her husband's behaviour and schedule. When she finds out what he is really like, she does a complete U-turn and helps Rachel. The reader also discovers Megan's doubts, wanderings and desire to charm any man she can in order to inject some excitement into her tedious daily routine. Above all, Rachel's idealised picture of Megan and Scott's relationship bears no resemblance to the reality and appears as a kind of trick, an imaginary gloss covering two people whose behaviour and aspirations are entirely at odds with those imagined by Rachel.

This means that the novel presents us with three viewpoints, three character arcs and three ways of understanding the story and the roles of each character based on their lives. The reader's questions change as the three women's outlooks on the world around them shift. For example, partway through the novel the reader finds themselves wondering how Rachel became an alcoholic, but by the end of the story a new question emerges: how could Rachel let herself be manipulated by her ex-husband? The novel features three variations on the same basic progression: the characters' self-discovery allows them to participate in an investigation not only into a murder, but also into their inner selves.

THE THRILLER

It is not the police investigation itself that forms the heart of the narrative, but rather the psychological development of the protagonists. The reader shares the anxieties, doubts and attempts to uncover lost memories that occupy the story's three female narrators. This means that we too are drawn into the story and flit between different viewpoints without being certain what is real and what is subjective.

We do not know any more than the characters, which allows us to identify with them. As such, when Rachel wakes up after being beaten up, realises that she was injured when she went to Witney on the evening of the murder and gradually recovers flashes of memory that show her that Tom was not alone in his car, the reader questions themselves just as the protagonist does, follows her reasoning and shares the same constant doubts. We are continually kept in suspense. Memories of the day of the murder come back to Rachel in flashes:

> "The woman I saw walking towards me a moment ago is just turning the corner; she's wearing a deep-blue trench wrapped around her. She glances up at the me as she passes and it's then that is comes to me: a woman... blue... the quality of the light. I remember: Anna. She was wearing a blue dress with a black belt [...]."
> (pp. 298-299)

But is this woman in blue really Anna, as Rachel thinks to begin with? The reader must wait until the end of the book to find out, as they are reliant on the narrator's hazy thoughts.

This narrative style, which gives the impression that the protagonists are in a state of constant tension, is characteristic of thrillers. This genre, both in literature and film, tries to maintain a high level of suspense in order to keep the reader (or viewer) on tenterhooks until the mystery is solved. In this novel, the mystery is complex, in particular due to the numerous red herrings that Rachel comes across when she is trying to make sense of her memories. In *The Girl on the Train*, elements of the thriller are combined with some of the characteristics of the detective novel, as a crime has been committed and Rachel investigates to try and get to the bottom of it.

The cliffhanger technique can be seen in the way the text is presented: the narrative constantly switches between the three characters, so it is not linear. The interweaving of three narrative threads results in constant breaks and delays the resolution of the plot. The suspense peaks when Rachel, having found out what Tom is really like, is facing him alone and covered in blood, while Anna stands by and seems reluctant to intervene in the violent dispute. However, this episode, which is narrated by Rachel, is interrupted by Anna's thoughts, leaving the reader believing that Tom is going to kill his ex-wife. The next chapter, which is narrated by Rachel, puts an end to the suspense by revealing that she kills him.

We can develop this categorisation further by saying that the novel has some of the features of the whodunit subgenre. This refers to stories in which the reader finds out clues at the same time as the characters carrying out the investigation and tries to solve the mystery themselves, ideally before a solution is given in the text. In *The Girl on the Train*, the reader uses the three interwoven points of view to try and make sense of the characters' reactions and assign each of them a role in the story, in order to identify the culprit.

This narrative technique often centres on precise key locations, where the majority of the events of the plot take place. In this novel, there are three important places: the train, where Rachel is alone with her thoughts, sometimes building an imaginary world, sometimes doubting her own perceptions and beliefs; Scott and Megan's house, which looks pleasant and charming from the outside but actually plays host to bitter arguments and acts of domestic violence; and the confined space of the bedroom of two couples, each one with the same male half, in the house shared first by Tom and Rachel, and then by Tom and Anna. This narrative technique developed in particular in English-language literature from the 1920s to the 1940s and is often used in thrillers.

THE TRAIN METAPHOR

Just as railways take travellers in one direction, from one fixed point to another, the lives of the novel's heroines have always stretched before them in a single direction. They are bound to their husbands or ex-husbands and have never challenged the information and behaviour prescribed by these men, to the point that they all let themselves be subjugated. In order to avoid rocking the boat, the female characters quickly become very passive. Consequently, Rachel, Anna and Megan never question what Tom tells them. They all believe that he is a good person, and although there are some signs that point to his shady behaviour, it takes them a long time to fully grasp the facts.

However, sometimes trains go off the rails and accidents happen. The monotonous rhythm that lulls passengers to sleep can quickly turn into cacophony, shock and catastrophe. The reader of *The Girl on the Train* experiences a similar change of trajectory and sudden accident. Although we cannot say that Rachel, Megan and Anna's lives were ever entirely calm, they were for the most part largely planned out. Rachel should have been a loving wife, a mother shut away in her Victorian house in a characterless neighbourhood just outside London. However, when she could not conceive a child, she slipped into alcoholism and, far from helping her to overcome her demons, her husband encouraged her so that she would have more blackouts and he could abuse her without her remembering what really happened. Of course, she has partially changed course: her train goes a bit further out of London, but the rhythm is the same and is punctuated by the same single desire, to get back together with Tom. When the train goes fully off the rails, when Rachel regains her ability to think and analyse what is happening around her, her trajectory takes a completely different turn and she is able to see things and people in a new light.

Similarly, it is as though Anna and Megan have been sedated for a long time because of the monotony of their journeys. Anna has fallen under Tom's spell and cannot wrap her head around the fact that he may not be as she imagined him. Megan, on the other hand, is afraid of her husband Scott and does everything she can to avoid incurring his wrath by following the plan he has set out for her life, but to no avail. However, they both come back to reality in the end: Anna to help Rachel after she kills Tom, and Megan when she decides to take her life into her own hands and stop letting men dictate her behaviour. In Megan's case, the train goes completely off the rails and ends up totally out of control, as she is murdered.

FURTHER REFLECTION

SOME QUESTIONS TO THINK ABOUT...

- Compare this novel with traditional detective stories. In what way is Paula Hawkins' writing different from the writing of Georges Simenon (Belgian writer, 1903-1989) or Agatha Christie (British writer, 1890-1976)?
- Hawkins' writing features different levels of focalisation. Explain.
- Does the precise, detailed dating of events reinforce the narrative's realistic dimension? Justify your answer.
- How does the author delay the discovery of the murderer and maintain the suspense?
- Is it fair to say that the novel constitutes an appeal on behalf of women in our society? Why?
- Is it possible to draw up a psychological portrait of Tom Watson, like a detective would do, and uncover some of his murderous tendencies?
- In your opinion, are the accidental death of Megan's baby and Rachel's alcoholism justi-

fiable? Build a case either for or against these characters.

- In what ways is this novel rooted in English society?
- Compare the characters of Rachel, Cathy, Megan and Anna. In what ways are they contrasting models of womanhood?
- Is the film adaptation of *The Girl on the Train* faithful to the content of the book?

We want to hear from you!
Leave a comment on your online library
and share your favourite books on social media!

FURTHER READING

REFERENCE EDITION

- Hawkins, P. (2016) *The Girl on the Train*. London: Transworld.

REFERENCE STUDIES

- Benvenuti, S. and Rizzoni, G. (1980) *The Whodunit: An Informal History of Detective Fiction*. New York: Macmillan.

ADAPTATION

- *The Girl on the Train*. (2016) [Film]. Tate Taylor. Dir. USA: Amblin Partners, DreamWorks, Marc Platt Productions, Reliance Entertainment.

www.brightsummaries.com

Ebook EAN: 9782808004503

Paperback EAN: 9782808004510

Legal Deposit: D/2017/12603/755

Cover: © Primento

Digital conception by Primento, the digital partner of publishers.